Shedding the Skin

My personal spiritual journey

By clairvoyant medium
Michael Dermeechi

THE CHOIR PRESS

Copyright © 2023 Michael Dermeechi

All rights reserved. No part of this publication may be reproduced or transmitted in any form or by any means, electronic or mechanical including photocopying, recording or any information storage or retrieval system, without prior permission in writing from the publishers.

The right of Michael Dermeechi to be identified as the author of this work has been asserted by him in accordance with the Copyright, Designs and Patents Act 1988

First published in the United Kingdom in 2023 by
The Choir Press

ISBN 978-1-78963-401-3

Contents

Acknowledgements	v
Chapter One: The awakening	1
Chapter Two: My eyes have been opened	4
Chapter Three: Food for thought	6
Chapter Four: Seek and you will find	9
Chapter Five: Look beyond	12
Chapter Six: My childhood years	19
Chapter Seven: Progression	24
Chapter Eight: The joy and fulfilment of working with the spirit world	26
Chapter Nine: Angels	45
Chapter Ten: Everything must pass, to be reborn	48
Chapter Eleven: There is still more we can learn	57

Acknowledgements

When I decided to write this book, it was for many reasons; first of all to share some of my philosophy to help others, who are starting out on their own spiritual journeys.

To find answers in their quest for the meaning of this life and to understand spiritual knowledge. Also, to look at any fears, doubts or problems from a spiritual point of view.

To show anyone can change if it's in their heart to do so and they want to, as eternal progress is open to every living soul.

So I would like to thank everyone who has played a part in my life, for without all of you I would not be the person I am today.

I would like to give thanks to all my spiritual teachers, who have inspired and guided me along a beautiful journey.

To Derek Marney, a wonderful human being and medium from Brighton, sadly passed in 2015.

To Freda Murphy, teacher friend and again a wonderful medium and very old school.

And to Anne and Michael Miles for their guidance.
To my son John Dermeechi and Rachel Johnston for their technical support.

Also to my beautiful fiancée, Michelle, for her support, love and guidance, who has played a big part in my spiritual growth, knowing or unknowing.

In the early years of my spiritual progression, I had many teachers who inspired me, guided me and gave me direction.

So I have only named but a few, the reason being they were all free from ego and inspired me in spiritual matters of truth, compassion and deep understanding, and I send my love and respect to them in the world of spirit, where I'm sure that they are carrying on their work.

So thank you with every piece of my heart to whoever buys a copy. And I hope this book uplifts, gives comfort and understanding.

Much love and blessings, Michael Dermeechi

Chapter One

The awakening

The awakening is like a snake shedding its old skin that serves no purpose anymore; you could say being born again, from the old to the new.

How does this come about? Well, it's when your inner spirit, that spark of the divine source, awakens deep inside us. Here are some reasons why and how this has taken place. It could be the loss of a loved one, your job, a hard life, some kind of abuse, be it sexual, mental or physical, or even just searching. Or maybe, like me, you did not like the person you were or became, or it could be even the simplest thing, such as someone coming into your life and opening your eyes, or perhaps you see an act of kindness and compassion, or even hear a kind word said or, yes, even a film that you have watched moves you, touching the very heart of you.

For me, my consciousness opened up because I did not like the person I was and the person looking back at me when I looked in the mirror. Up until then, it was all about me and no one else mattered; their views, their feelings did not count.

I was not only selfish but very controlling and manipulative and, I'm ashamed to say, a master of reverse psychology. Basically, I had all the traits I despise in a human being, which said a lot for me. I was my own worst enemy and everyone else's.

The change ...

I can only tell you how the change started within me and is still changing to this day, because it's not something that happens overnight. Like anything in life, it takes time to grow, little steps but always forward.

First for my growth came the lonely, dark hours at night, deep in thought reliving the past, feeling the pain of the people I hurt, putting myself in their shoes. Then the deep sadness, the guilt and the remorse. And, trust me, when you feel true remorse it takes no prisoners because it cuts deep into the very heart and mind, and you feel that you are yourself a prisoner of your own mind.

But don't get me wrong; I would not have had it any other way, because it needs to be real and felt deep inside.

But, being human, we are not perfect. There will be times of weakness; you might say a hurtful word or carry out a hurtful action, or even be a bit selfish, knowing or unknowing. When this happens, you will find you get upset and even angry with yourself, feeling perhaps you have failed in some way. (Don't.) Like I said, we are not perfect; we are human, and we make mistakes and can be weak. The key is to never give up, keep moving forward.

I find praying helps me. One thing I must explain: not everyone needs to inner cleanse or feel remorse; only people who walked the same path as the old me did. As many of you already have beautiful souls, it's just a case of connecting with your inner spirit, the divine spark of internal life.

How can I make the change?

First of all, we progress at different speeds. At first, we might be simply searching for spiritual truths, such as what is fact and what is simply word of mouth. I can only tell you from my own experiences. I read countless books and meditated and looked deep within, removing the bad stuff and keeping the good. Might I add that this included thoughts, but I can say this – I needed much healing because I was holding on to many hardships that occurred early on in my life and left me with many issues; as a result, completely changing my thought pattern.

This is about truth, so I'm not going to lie to you; I still have the odd negative thought, but life is about choices, so I chose simply at that time to delete them from my mind, instead of the old me acting on them. Okay, let me explain. Years ago, before I understood spiritual truths and knowledge, if someone wronged me, I would not have given a second thought to hurting them in some shape or form. But thank God that I see that is not the way. And I've learnt that what goes around comes around; that I can say for a fact.

Let me give you an example of when I tried to, and in some cases did, control people. In later years, I had the very same act done to me. You could say you certainly reap what you sow, and in truth, I hated having it done to me, but from a positive outlook I must say I needed to feel what it was like to understand how it must have affected the people to which I had done it, which in turn allowed me to educate people doing the same, show them how wrong it is and how it makes people feel. For one thing, it takes away their self-worth and confidence. Each experience in my life, good or bad, looking back, was so I can help people going through the same and to comfort and heal.

Chapter Two

My eyes have been opened

I have no doubt in my mind that life will not end when the physical body passes; the true spirit body lives on in the spirit world. Not only have I received proof, I have given proof that all man will return to the land of spirit. Looking back over my life, on the earth plane, I can see how we are sent here to learn lessons on how to live our lives in true harmony and understanding, both yours and others'.

Giving instead of taking, openness, turning everyday thoughts of hate into love, turning selfishness into compassion. One thing I have learnt in my life is that kindness breeds kindness and hate breeds hate, so by turning bad thoughts into good, loving thoughts, you have peace of mind and true harmony. Sometimes, we forget that God is love and we are all a spark of the great spirit. We tend to blame God when our lives sometimes seem to be painful or indeed sad, when loved ones pass or we lose a job, and when our girlfriend or boyfriend breaks our heart. These are just lessons we need to learn, work out, solve and move on from. However, never forget that our loved ones who have walked this earth before us and learnt many of their own lessons are close by and only too willing to help, if only we trust and believe they are around us and only a thought away, and are only too willing to help and guide us. One of the hardest things I found growing up was forgiveness, but with spirits' help, I have a greater understanding of life and how it works.

We can see all the beauty all around us in Mother Earth, the trees, the fields of green, the sand and sea, the mountains, and in the birds singing. Once, to me, a flower was no more than just a flower, but now I look into the flower at its wonderful array of colours, the shape and the delicate design of God's fine work of art. I rejoice at the four seasons, how in the autumn, Mother Nature begins her long winter sleep, the beautiful autumn colours of golden leaves, the burgundy orange and shades of brown. Then comes spring, bursting with new life buds and shoots popping up, an array of beauty and colour. And the April rain to quench Mother Earth's thirst. Summer is here once again with the beautiful sunshine beaming down, helping mankind to feel refreshed.

And, dear friends, let's not forget our beautiful spirit brothers and sisters of the animal kingdom, not just the ones we call domestic pets but also the animals in the wild. You may or may not agree with me, but I feel we can learn so much from them. Mankind has lost its way and is getting it so wrong with selfishness and greed and the lust for power. How many of us have had a bad day, and our ever-loving, ever-loyal dog has put their head in our lap, making us cheerful again? I have.

Chapter Three

Food for thought

In this chapter, I will explain how looking at life in a spiritual way can help us in our everyday lives view and understand problems and fears in a new light. I will be listing just a few subjects and showing a way of addressing them with a spiritual understanding. This way will really help you put them into perspective.

Number One: Patience

I'm sure, like me, whether queuing in a shop or bank, you're either in the middle or at the back of the queue – and the same could be said about being in a traffic jam – forever eager to be at the front, but when it comes to dying, we all want to be at the back of the queue. True? So does it really matter where in the queue in the shop or in the traffic jam we are? Patience truly is a virtue; everything comes to those who wait.

Number Two: Moving forward

We have all heard the saying, *one step forward, two steps back,* and at some stage in our lives, experienced this.

Okay, well, let's look at this with some spiritual wisdom. Think of the archer placing the arrow in the bow, then drawing it back, then letting go to propel it towards its target. So let's just introduce this into our way of thinking. One step forward, two steps back is the way it should be;

as we step back, we gather strength, wisdom and knowledge.

Many times, what holds us back is fear, coming out of our ever- safe and secure comfort zone, dipping our toes into the uncharted waters of the unknown, but please trust me on this; we cannot learn or grow or experience our full potential 'till we do so. When I left my comfort zone, I accomplished things that I myself never thought possible, just by changing my own thought pattern, and by doing so, opened many doors.

Number Three: Forgiveness

Forgiveness can be easy or hard, depending on how it is approached.

Why do I say this?

Well, there are two types of apology. First is the empty apology. This one has no meaning or depth about it, for in most cases it is just a get-out clause; in short, saving one's own skin so as not to face the music.

The second is the sincere apology, where a person (or persons) is full of remorse and wants to put the situation right, by both truth and honesty, and it is said with sincerity and comes from their heart.

With this kind of apology, both parties can be healed and can move on in true harmony.

Remember: we all have it in our hearts to forgive; all we need to do is apply it.

Number Four: Glass half empty or half full

A Ferrari will get you from A to B, but then so will a Mini.

Steak and chips will fill your stomach, but then so will a bowl of rice.

Champagne will quench your thirst, but then so will water.

Dear lord, I give thanks for the food in my fridge, for the roof over my head. I give thanks for the bed I sleep upon, the clothes I wear on my back. I give thanks for the fresh running water and heating that keeps me warm, my friends and my family.

Thank you, lord, for I'm truly blessed.

We should be thankful for what we have got, and worry not for what we have not.

I have met people who have so little in this life; however, they will share their food with you and give you their last penny.

They are true spiritual people in every sense of the word, hence the saying *poor but happy*.

But also I have met people with everything they desire, yet for some reason, that's not enough. They cannot satisfy their lust for the next bigger car, television, house. You name it, they must have it.

I saw a homeless man give half of what he had to another homeless man, who had nothing, without a thought for himself.

So I say, dear friends, let us rejoice in what God has given to us, and may we be thankful, Sometimes, the less you have, the more you have.

And sometimes, the more you have, the less you have.

There are two kinds of wealth, material and spiritual, and Jesus said that to worship God is not to worship money but to help the poor and the weak, and in his words, blessed be the poor.

Chapter Four

Seek and you will find

I was first introduced to spiritualism some years ago, not only by being a member of my own local spiritualist church but also sitting in a circle to develop my own mediumship and psychic skills, and proving this out on a church platform. Looking at the bigger picture, I know we all make mistakes in life. That's why we are here, to learn from them, so that's where forgiveness comes in, for the people we should forgive are only learning lessons, just as I am. So if I can forgive myself for my mistakes, is it not only right that I should forgive others? (Yes.) I can now look in the mirror and say, you know what, I like the person looking back at me.

If there is anything in this book you find hard to believe, that's fine, because some things that we experience in life are hard to explain or even understand, depending how far we have progressed on our spiritual path. But I can say, with my hand on my heart, that I would not insult your intelligence or embarrass myself in doing so. I believe everything that happens in our lives happens for a reason. I will say why and how I have come to this conclusion.

Twice, I have cheated death. The first time this happened, I was in a motorbike accident. And the second, I was running across a road without looking. I dodged the first car, but the next car, no doubt in my mind, should have taken my life on impact because of the speed of the car, but everything stood still. The next thing I knew I was on the other side of the road, thinking to myself, *how the hell did I get here?* (Was I helped by spirit?)

I believe in my heart, yes, I was. Why?

Perhaps maybe because of my life experiences, both good and bad, my happy-go-lucky, sometimes cheeky, personality, or perhaps my ability to uplift people with laughter, later to go on to become a medium where these skills would be called upon, so could it be I was saved for the job of working for the spirit world? Now when I work on behalf of the spirit world, I work on a high vibration of love and laughter, and please may I say not in a disrespectful way, as spirit is love and they want to see us joyful and happy, not sad, so they come to have their hearts lifted. The vibration I work with can change at any given time depending on the situation that I'm working on. I will explain why I say this.

I was conducting an evening of clairvoyance, for which a large part of the evening I was working on a high vibration which all of a sudden changed; it lowered. I looked into the crowd and said, in a low voice, 'Sir, please may I come to you?' He was an elderly gentleman, who had a great sadness in his eyes. I said, 'Sir, I have your wife with me,' after giving the gentleman clarification that without doubt I did have his wife with me.

I said, 'Sir, your wife is telling me to say to you that it's time for you to move forward with your life. However, you feel that if you do move on with life, in some way you would be betraying your wife's memory, and this makes you feel guilty as a result. Am I right, sir?'

'Yes,' was his reply.

'Well, sir, your wife is saying that had you, sir, passed before your wife, is it not true that you, sir, would want your wife to move forward and find happiness, and not think that life is over?'

He replied, 'Yes, I would want my wife to be happy and not sad.' With this, the gentleman burst into tears and said thank you.

Now, this gentleman needed to be in that church, so his dear wife could give him comfort and peace of mind.

I am now going to share with you all something beautiful that happened to me.

When working for spirit, we have feelings impressed upon us, such as how a person passed.

When I have someone who has passed over with a heart attack, I get a slight pain down my arm and a tightness in the chest area, but on one occasion it was different. Not only did I have the feeling of a heart attack ... (at this point, I must say that after we give clarification who the spirit was on the earth plane and how they passed over, spirit then takes that feeling away.) ... right, back to what I was saying, not only did I experience the feeling of the heart attack, but spirit allowed me to experience the actual passing.

Not at any stage did I leave my physical body, but I had the sensations, the feeling of my spirit leaving my body when passing over.

With this, I felt no pain or experienced any fear; only total peace and I felt surrounded by love.

Then turning to a lady in the congregation, I said, 'My darling, I have your husband here with me, and he passed from a heart attack.'

'Yes, you're right,' the lady said.

'And you have been worrying yourself silly that your husband suffered and was in pain?'

With tears in her eyes, she said, 'Yes, I have.'

'Well, fear no more as I have experienced your husband passing, and please trust me when I say this. It was a beautiful passing, no pain or fear, just a loving heavenly experience.'

With this, the lady thanked me and I moved on to the next recipient.

Chapter Five

Look beyond

Let me start this chapter with a powerful statement. *Don't judge a book by its cover.* And for this I will share with you all some of my family history, both true and fascinating, which helps blend this chapter together.

My great-grandfather, Mr John Alice, was born in Guinea, West Africa in 1833. In his twenties, he was taken from Guinea and sold into slavery, and taken to Rio de Janeiro, Brazil. His job was loading sacks of coffee onto ships, which are called brigs.

One day, he loaded a brig called *Alice* with its cargo of coffee on board. John hid in between the sacks of coffee on the brig, which was on its voyage back to England.

When John felt he was at a safe distance out at sea, he presented himself to the captain of the ship. And crew. The captain not only took John under his wing and treated him like a son, he gave him a job on board ship, and John became a part of the crew.

But he also gave him a name, because of the ship's log. So he called him John after his own Christian name, and his surname was to be Alice after the name of the ship.

After some time at sea, John settled in Falmouth, Cornwall, England. He met and married a local lady by the name of Elizabeth Jane Middleton Allen.

They had three children.

My great-grandfather became well liked in Falmouth, and I would say a bit of a celebrity in today's terms.

Now I owe it to the kind captain to share his name, for his kindness that after all this time feels our hearts with pride at being part of his life.

So God bless you, Captain John Truian of Penryn, because you could have sold Grandad John back to his owner. So, sir, you have truly earned your place in heaven. Sadly, my great-great grandfather passed in 1876, at the age of forty-three, in an accident on board a ship, leaving a widow and three children.

And to this day there has always been a John Alice, as my brother is called John Alice.

My grandad was his grandson, who married my Granny Ivy West, who was white, who had my dad, who was mixed race, who married my mother, who was white, so I am white in colour but both black and white in heart, and I am proud of my black roots.

So the moral of the story is did Captain John Truian judge a book by its cover? Thank God, no.

Now, that brings me to telling you about a dear friend of mine, called Peter. When we met, I had just moved into a flat and needed some milk, so I walked down to the local shop, to be greeted by Peter, a wonderful chap. We shook hands and I instantly felt a kindred spirit. Neither Peter nor myself saw colour or religion; we only felt respect for one another.

So there again is an illustration that a book's cover is not the story, only what will be found inside, for is it not what's inside that truly counts? By the way, my dear friend Peter is from India.

Sadly, many years ago, people felt that you were a bad lot if you had tattoos, or may have felt you were intimidating.

Going back to the early '80s, I applied for a job as a baker. Needless to say, the manager turned me down, saying I couldn't work there because I had tattoos, even after I reassured him that my tattoos would not fall into the cake mix. (I laughed.)

My great-great-grandad, who escaped slavery

The power of prayer

Question: are our prayers answered?

I can only answer this from my own experience in prayer and my own beliefs.

When I've asked for strength, God has given me strength.

When I've asked for hope, God has given me hope.

When I've asked for healing to be sent, God has sent healing.

When I've asked for courage, God has given me courage.
Ask yourself this: is your prayer for self-gain? Or is your prayer to help you or others in a non-self-gain way?

In my view, God answers all our prayers, sometimes not always the way we want it. But He is aware of what is right for us.

Prayer is also about giving thanks to God for the food we eat, the life we are given, our family and friends, the air, the sun, and Mother Earth herself. I said a prayer many years ago and forgot all about it. I asked God, please may the woman I grow old with be Asian. Well, like I said, I forgot all about it (laugh) and all these years later, my soulmate, the love of my life, is of Asian origin. Well, if that's not proof, I don't know what is. (Laugh.)

In my eyes, the power of prayer, with the right intention and with love in our hearts, is a gift from God.

Things happen in our lives. At first, they don't seem to make any sense, but as time goes on, you can see that there was a reason and a purpose, and it's then you can see God's plan unfold, and it's only then that it all makes perfect sense.

It may be a lesson that needed to be learnt or a part of your spiritual growth.

There are times when we are faced with challenges we think are beyond our reach and are not easy to achieve.

So let's look at it from this viewpoint.

A hill and a mountain: a hill is easier to climb than a mountain, but the view is not so beautiful. To climb a mountain takes longer and is much harder, but the view will be worth that extra effort.

For a moment, imagine the worst time of your life, thinking to yourself, *how am I going to get through this?* while you are in the depths of despair.

Well, looking back on it now, you did get through it, and maybe you're stronger, wiser and in a better place for it.

So think about it. That was the worst life could throw at you, so now you can see that we all worry far too much in life.

So get up, dust yourself down and move forward.

Okay, so let's talk about faith.

In my experience, faith has never let me down. If my van broke down in the sticks or I've been lost, faith has got me home safely.

If I've needed to complete a test of some kind, faith has been the key for completion of the test.

So, friends, have a little bit of faith in yourself and in whatever you're doing, because everything will turn out fine in the end.

And trust me when I say this: God will never leave you behind, as God will always answer your prayers.

Call on spirit when you need help, because if they can, and if it's in their power to do so, then they will only be more than happy to help you in your hour of need.

I will explain that by simply sending a thought out to my late father, help was at hand.

My biological father passed away nearly thirty years ago.

I did not really know him as he left the marital home when I was three years old, and that was the last time I saw him.

But sensing he's been in the spirit world, I'm glad to say that he is always at hand and only too willing to help me in any way he can.

Well, what I do know about my father is that he was good when it came to working on cars.

One day, I was trying to fix my car and was clueless and was getting very frustrated in what I was doing, so I sent a thought out to my father: *please help me, Dad.*

Well, he did not let me down. In two minutes flat, the car was fixed.

On another occasion, my sat nav stopped working in the middle of nowhere. Yes, I was totally lost.

So, again, I sent out a thought to my father, somehow in my mind, then I was being guided … turn right, drive a few miles, turn right again, turn left, etc. … then, yippee, my sat nav came on again. I was lost no more. Thanks, Dad.

I think it's true to say there's times when we tend to think the worst, so here is a story that may help when you think the worst instead of having faith.

Having a bad day? Have faith

A father passing by his son's bedroom was astonished to see that the bed was nicely made and everything had been picked up. Then he saw an envelope, propped up prominently on the pillow. It was addressed, Dad. With the worst premonition, he opened the envelope and, with trembling hands, read the letter ...

Dear Dad,

It is with great regret and sorrow that I'm writing this letter to you. I had to elope with my new girlfriend, because I wanted to avoid a scene with Mum and you, Dad. I've been finding a real passion with Stacy, and she is so nice, but I knew you would not approve of her because of all her piercings, tattoos, her tight motorcycle clothes, and because she is much older than I am.
But it's not only the passion, Dad. She's pregnant. Stacy said that we will be happy. She owns a caravan in the woods and has a stack of firewood for the whole of the winter. We share a dream of having many more children.
Stacy has opened my eyes to the fact that marijuana doesn't really hurt anyone. We'll be growing it for ourselves, and trading it with the other people in the commune for all the cocaine and ecstasy we want. In the meantime, we will pray that science will find a cure for AIDS, so Stacy can get better. She sure deserves it!

Don't worry, Dad, that I'm only fifteen. I can take care of myself.

Love, Paul

PS Dad, none of the above is true. I'm over at Gary's house. I just wanted to remind you that things could be worse. Ha ha.

Chapter Six

My childhood years

I was born Michael Alice in August 1963, in a small town called Gravesend in Kent.

My childhood was not a happy one by far. My mother, Kathleen, and my father, John, divorced when I was around three years old. My mother got married again, to Bill, who became my stepfather, when I was six years old. As for my real father, I never saw him again. I did track him down in my late twenties, but he had a new family and had moved on with his life so did not want to be bothered. He passed to spirit around twenty-seven years ago, but since being in the spirit world he has made up for this, and is always there when I need uplifting or support.

My upbringing was very strict at home and also at school.

I never knew what love was 'till I left home at the age of fifteen.

I'm not saying that I was not naughty at times, but the punishments were way over the top. That has stayed with me for all my life, and not in a positive way.

But saying that, there was no guide book on parenting back then. Looking back, they must have tried their best.

My school life started off well, as I was really happy in infants' and junior school, a welcome release from life at home.

Then came secondary school, a living hell from the age of eleven 'till fifteen, the worst years of my life.

It was a very strict all-boys school. From day one, I was bullied on a daily basis, by so many pupils, both physically and mentally.

I will just give you three examples.

One bully had got a pair of new steel toe cap boots and thought he would give the class a good laugh by kicking me in the testicles with full force. The more I cried out in pain, the funnier they thought it was.

On another occasion, a group of boys picked me up by my arms and legs and ran with me down the school playing field, so that my legs were apart, straight into the goal post; again, intense pain to my testicles.

How I ever became a father is beyond me.

Punching me in the back was also one of their favourite pastimes.

Right up until the day I left home, I wet the bed, too scared to tell my parents because of the punishment I would have received.

As a result, I would have to sleep in damp, wet pyjamas and bed sheets.

So going to school smelling of stale urine, and having a girl's name as a surname, made me an open target and good candidate for bullying.

On 25th May 1979, at the age of fifteen, I left school, and the next day I started my first day of work at Superdrug, free from the hell of school life.

I did have one good friend at school, called Mark Barker. He and his family became a big part of my life.

Mark and his family knew that I was not happy at home, so would invite me around for dinner and talk to me. They lived in a small flat and were waiting on the council to rent them a three-bed maisonette, and Mark's mother and father, John and Joyce Barker, said that when they moved, I could move in with them and be part of the family.

I had only been working in Superdrug a couple of days when Joyce and Mark's sister, Susan, came into the shop and said, 'We have got the maisonette. Would you like to move in?'

'Yes, please.'

So in May 1979, I had left school, started work and left home all within a couple of days at the age of fifteen.

And John and Joyce became like my foster parents, and helped me so much in my life skills.

I felt loved, wanted and part of a family.

Sadly, both John and Joyce have passed away but are always in my thoughts and heart.

My relationship with my mother and stepfather, Bill, improved over the years, but sadly they also passed a few years ago and are very much in my thoughts and heart too.

So what happened to me, who left school, home and started work all at the tender age of fifteen? Well, to tell you the truth, I strayed off the path, let's say. I found myself in some dark avenues, so I had a choice. I knew if I stayed in my home town, I would either end up in prison or dead, because I was on a downward spiral. So for my own sake, I changed my surname from Alice to Dermeechi and moved to the West Country, got a job and started a new life; a new me.

I must say at this point that I was still making mistakes, and it was years later that I found the true spiritual self that I am today.

However, I truly believe the mistakes I made along the way were to help and guide people who are walking the same dark path I once walked before them.

Now I feel I can guide them out of the darkness into the light.

So I do feel that my past had a meaning and a purpose.

Also, I became a youth worker, a qualified mentor, and worked for the youth offending team, until the government made budget cuts.

As for the bullying, that's a thing of the past, as I took up various forms of martial arts and, to my surprise, I became West Midlands champion, at the age of forty, so I learnt to stand up for myself and for those people that are themselves being bullied. Everything in life has an opposite. There may be low points in our lives, but there will also be high points. So I say this to you all: don't let your yesterday take away your tomorrow, as your darkest days will give you strength.

Words can be very powerful, so here is what I feel we need to remember:

Be mindful to taste your words before you release them, for if they taste bitter then keep them within.

A simple compliment or a kind word can change a person's day from a bad one to a good one, just by uplifting or even inspiring. We can give strength and hope.

Our words can also have an everlasting effect, both on ourselves and others. For example, words can prevent a war, start a war, or even end a war.

Our words carry enormous weight, more than we sometimes realise.

They often impact people for many decades, providing the courage to press on, or one more reason to give up. And here is my spiritual view of the true meaning in the word *love:*

Someone once asked me, how can you love someone who does not love you? My reply was easy. I said, 'Love is not about self; that's ego talking. Love comes from the love you feel for others, caring about how they feel, their wellbeing and their spiritual growth.'

I'm not saying that it's wrong to love oneself, but simply to put others before self.

There are many facets when it comes to love.

For example, the love we have for a husband or wife, the love we have for our children, or friends. But whatever type we are referring to, if it comes from your heart with sincerity and without want, then that is real love.

In my life, I have felt love from friends, family and a partner, but never have I felt such a rich and pure love as I have felt from the spirit world. Divine love from the spirit world is powerful and emotional at the same time; it wraps itself around you, filling you with healing energy.

So powerful is this love that I myself have burst into tears, for it is intense, and fills your heart with joy, peace and true contentment. The truly wonderful thing about love is that we can't buy or sell it, but we can give it freely in abundance, all that your heart can give.

And what you give out comes back tenfold.

Love is the spiritual home of kindness, compassion and empathy. It will also uplift us and fill us with happiness and contentment.

Chapter Seven

Progression

Has man progressed forwards or backwards throughout time? Sadly, I conclude in my view we have not progressed enough. Why do I say this? I will explain why I have come to this conclusion.

Back in the time of the Roman Empire, the weak and the vulnerable were used for their entertainment, by the use of bloody force. And today this is still a part of life, but using a different method, such as reality television, where again the weak and vulnerable are put on public display for man's entertainment, admittedly not by force, but still with the same means, resulting, in some cases, in low self-worth, depression, anxiety and, in certain cases, leading to taking one's own life. This is just one example. I will point out a few more where change is very much needed.

The Co-operative Society was destined to be different, and was started by the Rochdale pioneers in 1863 to help the poor, by establishing an economical way of shopping; however, today, not so cheap; a fine example where materialism has been put before spiritual kindness.

The same can be said about religion. Even in these modern times, many are being persecuted, imprisoned and even executed for their religious beliefs.

Which in my view makes a mockery out of religion. Also, in some countries, freedom of speech is suppressed with the fear of imprisonment or death. Was it not Jesus who said, two thousand years ago, let he who is without sin cast the first stone, as a woman was to be stoned for adultery? Yet, today, people in Middle Eastern countries are still being put to death for being gay and for committing adultery.

Quote me if I'm wrong, but is it not a greater sin to take another person's life, because such barbaric punishments seem hypocritical to my way of thinking. What I say is, let us take one word from all of the different religious faiths, and let that word be *love*. Let us use this single word as the foundation to build a better world for the use of all.

Because where there is love, we will find kindness, compassion, tolerance, understanding and acceptance. Let us love beyond words. Amen.

It is said that heaven is a beautiful place, so let's try to make earth just as beautiful, turning hate into love; selfishness into kindness; give more, take less; compromise; be more understanding and tolerant and mindful of our actions and words towards each other; to live side by side in love, peace and harmony.

Chapter Eight

The joy and fulfilment of working with the spirit world

Working for the spirit world is not only an honour and a privilege, but it's also mind-blowing and full of surprises. In this chapter, I will explain what I mean.

Our loved ones in the world of spirit are far more advanced and clever than we are, and will use many methods to make contact with those left on the earth's plane, to give proof that life does not end when the spirit leaves the physical body.

This they can do through a medium, be it physical, trance or mental mediumship, or even through signs. Ever turned on the radio thinking of your loved one and a record has come on that has meaning for both of you, a memory you both shared, or you are worried about something and at that very moment a white feather appears at your feet?

When I'm working with spirit, they not only put thoughts into my mind (this is when trust comes into play); they're not my thoughts but the work of spirit.

They will use my memory bank, sometimes past experiences and even my own loved ones in spirit, about which I will explain more as I write this chapter.

Also, they will use my sense of smell, hearing and sense of feeling, both emotional and physical.

I got a phone call one evening from a young lady who asked me if I would come and give her mother, who had not long left to live, a private reading.

I said, 'Of course I will,' and booked her mother in for the next evening.

Now, as I said, spirit works in many ways. On this occasion, they used what I call the puzzle effect, where nothing seems to make sense at first, but it builds up to form the bigger picture and all makes perfect sense in the end.

So, the next evening, I took the short drive over to their house.

The daughter greeted me and thanked me for coming to see her mother, who was sat at the kitchen table, at such short notice.

After settling myself, spirit showed me a picture of a tiger. I thought, *how strange*. Now this is when spirit taps into my memory bank. 'My dear, spirit is showing me a tiger, and you don't look like a zookeeper,' I said, laughing.

I said, 'The only way I can think of this is, when I was a child, I used to watch *Coronation Street* and there was a man called Billy Walker, who was dating a woman called Deirdre Langton, whom he liked to call *Tiger*.'

With this, the lady burst out laughing. She said, 'OMG, I know a friend in spirit called Billy Walker.'

Then I was aware that there was a little girl with me. I said, 'My dear, can you take a little girl in the spirit world? She is around seven years old, with long blonde hair. She passed in an accident.'

Her reply was no.

'Okay,' I said. 'Remember that I have said that.'

Then I went on to say, 'Can you take the name Stanley?'

'No,' was her reply again.

I said, 'Don't worry, I will carry on.'

Suddenly I was being taken to a house. As I stood outside, I felt heartache and depressed and did not have any desire to enter the building, but I knew I had to.

As all this is taking place, I'm telling the lady all that I'm seeing and feeling. 'OMG,' she said, 'yes, I can take the little girl and the name Stanley and that very house.'

She went on to explain everything. She said the house was in Liverpool and Stanley was the name of the street the house was in.

There lived a little girl who died. One day, her brother was carrying her on his shoulders when he tripped down the stairs and the little girl landed at the bottom of the stairs and died.

So can you see how, with the puzzle effect, all parts fit together in the end?

Here we have spirit making contact by way of a song. I will explain how this came about.

I was doing a clairvoyant evening in Gloucestershire, when in the interval I needed to use the bathroom. All of a sudden, I heard singing in my thoughts. The following words were sung: *Up town, leader of the city, the back of my neck is getting dirty.*

When I went in, I was aware that the spirit I had with me was a dustman when on the earth plane, with a very funny sense of humour, and the words *back of my neck is getting dirty* was his funny way of saying he was a dustman.

Now, on this occasion, spirit gave me one word and it built up from there.

I told this lady that spirit just said, *snakebite*. Now I knew straight away it was the drink called snakebite, and said, 'My dear, you had a close friend who passed who shared a love of snakes with you?'

'Yes,' she said. 'That's very true.'

So by just one word, spirit started the ball rolling.

Spirit also gives you feelings about how a person has passed.

I was doing a charity night for Macmillan Cancer Support. As I sat there waiting to go on, I felt like a block of ice, really cold. I got up and said to this man, 'Sir, you have a friend in spirit who passed from hypothermia. He went out drinking and never made it home. Am I right, sir?'

'Yes,' he replied, 'that's correct.'

On this next occasion, spirit worked both with myself and my grandfather, for this next link.

I told this black lady in the congregation that my own grandfather was standing next to me, and spirit wanted me to describe him and how he passed, before her own grandfather came in, just for extra proof.

I said, 'My dear, my grandfather was around five feet two inches tall, very broad across the shoulders and very rounded around the tummy area, and had a real gruff, deep voice. He was black in colour, a farmer, and passed over very quickly from a heart attack.'

I said to the lady, 'Does this make sense to you?'

Her reply was, 'Yes, I can take all you have said, but, sir, you are white and I am black, so how can our grandfathers be the same colour?'

After laughing, I said, 'My dear, my grandfather married a white lady, so my father is mixed race who married a white woman, so I'm quarter mixed race.'

But it just shows you how spirit works in many ways.

What I'm going to talk about now is working with spirit energy. We are energy and everything in this and the world of spirit is made up of pure energy.

As we are all aware, a man has a masculine energy and a female has a feminine energy, and I feel these different energies when making a connection with spirit.

But, saying that, someone who was gay while on the earth plane can come across as a feminine energy.

However, this is not a problem as we will be talking, blending our thoughts together, while we are working together.

Also, a mother's energy can be felt in a more loving way.

One thing I must point out is that when we leave the earth plane, we are who we were and still are. Let me explain: if you swear on the earth plane, then you will still be the same in the spirit world, until you feel no need to swear anymore.

If you smoked on the earth plane, I will smell your tobacco when working with you.

While working with spirit, I have felt their emotions. I have burst out laughing and burst out crying and felt love beyond words.

So now you can see that working for the spirit world is truly a blessing from God.

How I perceive passing over, or, to put it into earthly terms, death:

Well, life and death go hand in hand. You cannot have one without the other.

Doesn't matter what age it happens, but we will all face it at some point.

Tell me, when you were in your mother's birthing canal, were you afraid to be born? No, of course not, so why be afraid to be born again into a beautiful new world we call the spirit world?

Treat death the same as life itself: an adventure.

When trying to understand life, I think it's good sometimes to read between the lines, and what better way to do this than by popping in a few stories that have meaning and are thought-provoking. Please enjoy.

To be beautiful, you don't have to be handsome or pretty; you only need to have a beautiful heart full of love and compassion and kindness.

I have always said, the more you put in, the more you get out of whatever you're doing.

Put your heart and love into your work and it will pay off one day.

Here is a story for when we forget to put our hearts into our work.

There was a builder, and he was the best in his field of work. Now, this builder would build one house a year for his boss.

He would use the best and most expensive materials he could buy, and would put all his time and love into building a fine house.

However, he was growing old and tired, so he said to his boss, 'When I've finished building this house, I'm going to retire.'

A couple of months passed by and the house was completed, so the builder was handing over the keys to his boss when his boss said, 'Please can you build one more house, just one, before you retire?'

With a disappointed look, he reluctantly agreed, but this time he used the cheapest materials and he sure did not put his heart or love into building the house.

Six months later, he had finished building the house, in half the time he would spend lovingly building houses beforehand.

So now this was done and he gave the keys to his boss.

With that, the boss said, 'They are your keys to your new home, a present from me for all the hard work and wonderful fine houses you have built me.

A beautiful heart

One day, a young man was standing in the middle of the town, proclaiming that he had the most beautiful heart in the whole valley.

A large crowd gathered and they all admired his heart, for it was perfect.

There was not a mark on it.

Yes, they all agreed, it truly was the most beautiful heart they had ever seen.

The young man was very proud and boasted more loudly about his beautiful heart.

Suddenly an old man appeared at the front of the crowd and said, 'Why, your heart is not nearly as beautiful as mine.'

The crowd and the young man looked at the old man's heart.

It was beating strongly ... but it was full of scars ...

It had places where pieces had been removed and other pieces put in, but they didn't fit quite right, and there were several jagged edges.

In fact, in some places, there were deep gouges where whole pieces were missing.

The people stared. *How can he say his heart is more beautiful?* they thought.

The young man looked at the old man's heart and saw its state and laughed.

'You must be joking,' he said. 'Compare your heart to mine, but mine is perfect and yours is a mess of scars and tears.'

'Yes,' said the old man, 'yours is perfect-looking, but I would never trade with you.

'You see, every scar represents a person to whom I have given my love.

I tear out a piece of my heart and give it to them, and often they give me a piece of their heart, which fits into the empty place in my heart, but because the pieces aren't exact, I have some rough edges, which I cherish, because they remind me of the love we shared.

'Sometimes, I have given pieces of my heart away, and the other person hasn't returned a piece of his heart to me.

These are the empty gouges. Giving love is taking a chance.

Although these gouges are painful, they stay open, reminding me of the love I have for these people too, and I hope someday they may return and fill the space I have waiting.

'So now do you see what true beauty is?'

The young man stood silently with tears running down his cheeks.

He walked up to the old man, reached into his perfect, young, beautiful heart and ripped a piece out.

He offered it to the old man with trembling hands.

The old man took his offering, placed it into his heart, and then took a piece from his old scarred heart and placed it into the wound in the young man's heart.

It fit ... but not perfectly ... as there were some jagged edges.

The young man looked at his heart, not perfect anymore but more beautiful than ever.

Since love from the old man's heart flowed into his, they embraced and walked away, side by side.

Create a life that has both purpose and meaning

Whether you are a teacher, lawyer or doctor, whatever profession you are in, master your craft. Do it to the best of your ability and put your love into it.

For the more you put into your profession, the more you will get in return. This also applies to your family life.

When I took up the role of being one of God's many messengers, proving there is life beyond the grave, I made sure that I mastered my craft, never missing a training circle, and having a willingness to learn, so that when I'm giving a message from someone in the spirit world to their loved one on the earth plane, it is clear and precise and without doubt.

For it is very important to bear in mind that words can make or break a person, how you put the message across, because you want to give upliftment, not leave someone feeling depleted.

The same applies to spiritual advice and guidance, and also to sharing spiritual knowledge with those who seek answers.

Okay, so perhaps the burning question many of you would like answered is can anyone become a medium? Well, the simple answer is yes. I will tell you the reason why. First, let me say this, I'm nobody special, just an everyday run-of-the-mill man. I'm also dyslexic and I have Asperger's, a disorder which is a form of autism, and it has never held me back.

What is important to remember here first is that we are all spirit, so, in short, it is one spirit connecting to another spirit.

And everyone has that ability; it's just a case of knowing how to. Every one of us is psychic, even if you do not know it.

Okay, let me explain. Have you ever walked into a room and felt a good or bad atmosphere, or just sensed when someone is happy or sad? Well, that is called picking up on someone's energy.

My advice is to join a spiritualist church open circle, to learn and understand how to connect to the spirit world in a safe way.

But don't rush, and learn and work from the heart and in love and light.

Stay humble and free from ego, don't sit in the circle for a couple of weeks and say, okay, I'm a medium now. Wrong!

To do it right will take you years of discipline and hard work before you are ready.

And even when you are ready, there will be more to learn.

I've seen so many times someone sitting in the circle for a couple of weeks, then giving out business cards, trying to make fast money from private readings. Being undertrained can do more damage than good; never put money over service.

Being one of God's workers should not have to come with a price. Give yourself and your time freely, as reward is the love of service.

Having a positive attitude

Every day, when I wake up, I have a choice: to have a good or a bad day. So I choose to have a good day, no matter what lays ahead, just like the lady with a positive attitude to life in this story.

There was once a woman who woke up one morning, looked in the mirror and noticed she had only three hairs on her head.

'Well,' she said, 'I think I'll braid my hair today.'

So she did and she had a wonderful day.

The next day, she woke up, looked in the mirror and saw that she had only two hairs on her head.

'Hmm,' she said, 'I think I'll part my hair down the middle today.'

So she did and she had a grand day.

The next day, she woke up, looked in the mirror and noticed that she had only one hair on her head.

'Well,' she said, 'today, I'm going to wear my hair in a ponytail.'

So she did and she had a fun day.

The next day, she woke up, looked in the mirror and noticed that there wasn't a single hair on her head.

'YEAH,' she said, 'I don't have to fix my hair today.'

You have two kinds of wealth: spiritual wealth and material wealth. Pick wisely.

This story will help you decide.

There was a king who lived in a big castle on top of a hill.

Down the bottom of the hill lived a family of peasant farmers; a husband, his wife and son.

One day, the king saw a priest walking by his castle. He called out to the priest. 'Come, I need to ask you something,' he said. 'Tell me, I'm wealthy beyond my dreams, I can buy anything I want, the best food, best wine, best clothes, but I'm sad, unfulfilled and miserable.

'But take a look at that peasant family at the bottom of the hill. They are happy, joyful, laughing and having fun. Yet they are poor.

'Priest, please tell me why this is so.'

The priest said it was because they didn't belong to the ninety-nine club.

The king replied, 'Tell me, Priest, what is the ninety-nine club?'

With that, the priest said, 'Give me ninety-nine gold coins, and I will be back in one month's time to show you why you are so unhappy and they are blissfully happy.' With that, the king handed him the gold coins and the priest went on his way.

Later that night, the priest left the bag of gold coins outside the front door of the peasant family's home.

The next morning, the peasant husband found the bag of gold coins and looked into the bag, and in a fit of rage he said, 'There are only ninety-nine gold coins in this bag. It's going to take me a year to make one gold coin to make it up to a hundred.'

The next day, he looked in the bag and there were only ninety-eight gold coins in the bag. He started arguing with his wife. 'Where has the gold coin gone?' he shouted at her. She said that they needed supplies.

From that day on, all they did was argue and bicker and shout.

One month had passed and the priest presented himself to the king.

Well,' the king asked him, all confused, 'why is that once-happy family so unhappy now?'

The priest replied, 'Because now they have joined the ninety-nine club.'

The moral of the story is, the more you have, the more you want.

The less you have, the more you have.

The proof is in the pudding. Look at all the married couples who have won the lottery. How many are still together? Not many. How many still have their wealth? Again, not many.

So is it not wiser to have spiritual wealth rather than material wealth?

Don't be too quick to judge

With understanding, judgement ceases to exist. For it is man's lack of understanding that means judgement exists.

I will give you an example.

You see a woman of the night at the end of the street. Now, the first thought is prostitute ... dirty ... disease ... unclean ... and maybe worse, thinking the vile word whore.

And, straight away, judgement has been passed without understanding.

Now let's look at this from a loving heart without judgement but with compassion and understanding.

Ask yourself this: why is she selling her body?

Could it be she has been kidnapped against her will, from a foreign land, and they have her passport and are threatening to harm her family back home?

Could it be she is so poor that she needs to feed her young children? Is that not a mother's love, not to let her children starve?

Could it be she fell in love with the wrong man, who got her dependent on hard drugs?

Could it be she was raped and so badly abused as a child, or even as an adult, that she has lost her self-worth, both for herself and her body?

And now the men who use her body, as if it was just a piece of meat, have a wife and children at home, spending the housekeeping for their own sexual gratification, with the added bonus of giving their wife or partner a sexually transmitted disease, or perhaps, even worse, a death sentence.

So before passing judgement on the poor soul, let us try a little bit of compassion and understanding, because it is someone's mother or daughter.

As I have written in this book, my childhood years were a very unhappy time for me, due to treatment at the hands of bullies. I must have had some inner strength to be here and writing this today. As for my dear friend Leroy, he was not so strong and took his own life.

What I can say about my dear friend is that he was life itself, both loving and kind, and I'm sure he will be in the spirit world, educating the minds of bullies that it is wrong.

So I dedicate these wise words I'm about to write in his memory. God bless you, Leroy, for your friendship and kind spirit.

So, dear friends, next time a person puts you down or makes you feel worthless, show them this ... what I'm going to simply call *Think first.*

Think first

The girl you just called fat ... She's on diet pills.

The girl you just called ugly ... She spends hours putting make-up on, hoping people will like her.

The boy you just tripped ... He is abused enough at home.

See the man with the ugly scars ... He fought for his country.

The fourteen-year-old girl with the kid, that you just called a slut ... She got raped.

That guy you just made fun of for crying ... His mother is dying.

People already have enough sorrow to deal with; please don't give them any more just because you want to crack a joke.

Cause and effect

All life, both on the earth and in the spirit world, is governed by a natural universal law.

God's law, not man's.

A law that goes hand in hand with the free will God has allowed us, to make decisions to a degree.

Okay, so what is the meaning of cause and effect? Well, in short, it is a result of something after an event, which I will explain in more detail.

Cause equals a spoken word, a thought or an action that has taken place.

Effect equals a result of consequences, or the aftermath, good or bad, after a spoken word, thought or action.

I will list a couple of examples where cause and effect have materialised.

Example one:

Someone is driving along a country lane, at night or in the daytime; the result will be the same.

When speeding to get to their destination, suddenly they find themselves behind a tractor or lorry on a blind bend. In a moment of stupidity, they decide to overtake the vehicle in front. At the same time, a vehicle is coming the opposite way.

Then bang! Both hit head-on.

Resulting in the driver of the oncoming vehicle being killed outright.

Resulting in loss of life, and a wife without a husband, and children without a father, and parents without a son.

So, through a lack of patience, a whole family is affected by one's actions.

So, cause was the actions of lack of patience.

Effect: loss of life and the after-effects of leaving a family devastated as a result.

Always drive to arrive safely.

Example two:

A lad and a few of his friends go out drinking one night. The lad has way too much to drink and thinks he can take on the world.

Showing off to his friends, he decides to pick a fight with whomever he can.

With one single punch, he hits a man who falls back and hits his head on the kerb.

Resulting in the man he punched ending up on a life support machine, with severe brain damage.

After twelve long agonising weeks, with his family around his bedside, they're told by the doctors that there is no hope left.

So, with heavy hearts, it's decided the life support machine should be turned off.

So, cause was a dad getting drunk and punching a man for no good reason.

Effect: loss of a life and devastation of a loving family, and a long prison sentence for the action of a drunken moment of madness, resulting in two wrecked families.

Example three:

Jesus carried the cross on his back for all our sins.

The heavy cross I carry on my back is for my sins, of yesterday, fall of remorse and a heavy heart, for the selfish person I once was.

But, thank God, I saw the light, by changing my thought pattern and my actions.

Cause equals the way I treated people.

Effect equals how it made them feel.

Remember karma; what goes around comes around, like a boomerang.

Boomerang

"Some people may call it karma,
But one thing I've come to know
Is that we only reap in life
Whatever it is we sow

Although we try to follow
The planned course that we have charted,
So very often the finish line
Is the same place where we started

They say history repeats itself,
And if this statement is true
Then good things you do for others
Will always come back to you
The blessings may not be instant
Or not even recognised

Or they may take many years to be truly realised
When you perform an act of kindness,
It is never unrequited
For there will always come a time
When you two are reunited.

Let these blessings we receive
In the days that we are living
Be not the reason for this kindness,
But rather the joy we feel in giving

We're all in this life together
Sharing the world with one another
And so it is we help ourselves,
Each time we help each other

If caring is not your priority
And your compassion is nil
And you're convinced your life on earth
Is just the void that you fill

You may need someone's help
Before this earthly life you leave
And you'll be sorry if what you've given
Is then, what you'll receive
For like the endless ocean waves
That steadily roll to the shore
Or the predictable route
Of a revolving door

Like the endless rhyming lyrics
Of a childhood song that you sang,
Your life's actions will come back to you
Just like a boomerang..."

So I've explained the negative side of cause and effect.

Now there is a positive side. That is, can you imagine just how a simple smile can change a person's day, from a bad to a good day.

Can you imagine how spending time with someone who is lonely lifts their day.

Giving way to someone on the road.

Shopping for someone who can't get out of their home.

Listening to someone's problems, just being there. Plus, it's a fact that you learn more by listening than you do by talking.

Here is a beautiful piece of work written by the late Spike Milligan.

Smiling

"Smiling is infectious,
You catch it like the flu
When someone smiled at me today,
I started smiling too.
I passed around a corner
And someone saw my grin.
So when I smiled,
I realised I'd passed it on to him.
I thought about that smile, and then I saw its worth,
Because a single smile like mine can travel around the earth.
So if you feel a smile begin don't leave it undetected.
Let's start an epidemic quick and get the world infected."

Lessons in life

To make a difference in life, to bring us happiness and fulfilment, and self-worth, all we need to do is think, *are my words, thoughts and actions hurting anyone, or are my words, thoughts and actions inspiring or uplifting anyone?*

For a kind word or advice, or simply an ear, can make a person's day.

Let us spend less time judging, and instead let's spend more time loving and showing compassion and understanding.

Let us all be mindful and wise, before we release our words. Let's all taste them, and if they taste bitter, let's not release them.

However, should they taste sweet, let them flow with love and kindness.

Let's give our time, and make time, for those who need it most, asking for nothing in return, for your reward is just that. You helped someone; that is all the reward one needs.

If someone is hungry, set them a place at your table.

If someone needs clothes, give them the shirt off your back, the shoes off your feet, for their need might be greater than yours.

If someone needs shelter, make up a spare bed.

The world that we live in can be a beautiful place for everyone, if we open our hearts and share what we have, instead of, I want more; I cannot part with this and that because I will have less.

But I say this, dear friends (which is only a thought), as most of the time we have more than we ever need, and indeed waste so much, when there are souls out there with nothing; no food, no home, not knowing where the next meal is coming from, going without so their young can eat that day.

If we end greed and lust for power, and we learn to share, then we will put an end to human suffering, if we all play our part and just think before we act.

Never offer the kind of help that disempowers a person. Encourage the empowerment of people. Disempowerment equals dependency.

Chapter Nine

Angels

My late mother, Kathleen, would talk a lot about angels and her love for them.

Before we are born into this world, a guardian angel is assigned to be by our side, to help guide and protect us, from birth to the grave, and to take us back to heaven, when our soul leaves our earthly body.

Your guardian angel is a gift from God to help you throughout your time on earth and beyond.

And your guardian angel does not judge you but loves you unconditionally.

I will give you two examples of where my guardian angel helped me.

One Friday afternoon, I was driving home from work, when a voice in my head said *slow down*. Thank God I listened as two minutes later a dog ran out in front of my car, which clipped the dog, but thank God it was fine and ran off.

The second time was when I myself was running across the road, paying no attention; I was in my own little world. I ran out into the road. I knew the first car would miss me, but the second car should have taken my life, at the speed it was going. However, time seemed to just stop. The next thing I remember is being on the other side of the road, thinking that the car, by rights, should have hit me head-on.

Thank you, my dear guardian angel friend.

Getting to know your guardian angel?

Well, first of all, let me make this point, so you can have a better understanding.

Your guardian angel and your loved ones in the spirit world can only come forward and help and guide you if you ask and give permission, as you have been given free will by God.

And also remember that they cannot live your life for you.

When making contact with mine, I asked his name, and the first name that entered my mind was Peter.

Okay, to verify this, I used my crystal pendulum, clockwise for yes, and anticlockwise for no. My answer was yes, so Peter is his name.

Again, let me point out that it is always important to make yourself safe while working in this way, which I do by saying a prayer.

You may wish to ask for a sign, which might be you finding a white feather. You may see your lights flicker, or you may keep seeing the same number, or even numbers, hear a song or have a dream or recall a memory.

So basically I have given you a seed, so seek and you will have a much better understanding, because my knowledge of angels is in its early stages.

So what I will say is look for a book called *Angels in my Hair* by Lorna Byrne.

And this lady not only sees angels, but her knowledge is interesting, helpful and uplifting.

Angels, just like us, were made by God, but unlike us, they have not been incarnated to the earth plane.

The sole purpose of their creation is to serve God by carrying out His work, helping mankind.

So when we say a loved one who has passed has become an angel, now looking after us, this is not quite true; the spirits of our loved ones do not become angels, but it is true that our loved ones will indeed look out for us, and will try to help us, just like our guardian angels.

But please understand that a spirit and an angel are two different beings.

A spirit is a soul who has lived on earth; an angel has not lived on the earth plane.

However, angels can walk among us while doing God's work.

The highest angels are your archangels, which are, you could say, God's generals, who oversee the angels' work, and also have their own duties.

Chapter Ten

Everything must pass, to be reborn

Life is a cycle ... of life, death and rebirth. As with nature.

Come autumn, the leaves on the trees fall and die as nature sleeps and awakes refreshed and reborn in the spring.

As so will and does mankind. From the day we are born into this world, there will be a time we all must leave it, to be reborn into another dimension that we call heaven or, as I like to say, the world of spirit.

We all have a day, a time and a place, and a reason when we pass over.

We don't know when or how this will take place, but if my spiritual beliefs and understanding are correct, then we are in for a beautiful experience.

I say this to you all: have any of you seen a depressed caterpillar? No, because it knows it's going to turn into a beautiful butterfly and be free.

As we will ... to be free of the suffering of health and earthly worries, into a new world full of love and understanding and beauty.

Now, just like in the supermarket, where everything has a sell-by date, we also have a sell-by day we must pass.

But like an apple falling from a tree, this will only happen when the time is right, when the apple is ripe.

So, in other words, you may be in [a ...] passengers, three die, and you survive.

You may try and end your life in som[e...] hospital; the list is endless.

What I'm saying is, if it's not your time to p[ass, it] will not take place.

However, if it is time, then you will leave your earthly body.

I will now set out an example of when it's not your time, in the case of what happened one day when it was not Johnny Rotten's time.

21st December 1988.

John Lydon, band name Johnny Rotten of the punk band the Sex Pistols, and his wife, Nora Foster, were due on Pan Am flight 103, which was blown up by terrorists over Lockerbie, Scotland. All 259 passengers on board lost their lives, and also eleven people on the ground lost their lives.

They were booked on Pan Am flight 103 but missed the flight because John's wife, Nora, took too long packing, so they decided to go back to bed.

When they woke up, after watching the news and receiving phone calls from friends and family, they just looked at each other and almost collapsed, after hearing what had happened.

A clear indication that it was not their time to leave this world.

However, if it is your time to leave this earth plane, remember that this death is not a punishment; it is a liberation.

As we are all aware, from the day we are born into this world, we know there must be a time when we must leave it.

Here is another example. One night, both my friend and I decided to go for a walk. Well, across the road from where we lived in Gravesend was a promenade by the River

...es. It was the middle of winter, with snow on the ground.

My friend said to me, 'Hey, Michael, there is a body over there, lying in the snow.' So we walked over to the body and were shocked to see it was my brother John, lying in a pool of sick, so I quickly turned him on his side, to make sure he was still alive.

Then I took him back home with us to sober him up. Had we not turned up at that time, had we not gone out for a walk, then I'm sure my brother would definitely have passed, from choking on his own sick, or hypothermia. So, again, it was not his time to pass.

But for many, fears set in; when and how will I pass, will it hurt, etc.?

Well, I say this: how many of you have seen a caterpillar looking depressed? And I'm sure the answer will be nobody, as a caterpillar knows it will turn into a beautiful butterfly, and just like the caterpillar, you too will become a better version of yourselves, you could say, from cotton to silk.

If you could imagine planning for a holiday, which is full of adventure and excitement at the wonderful things to look forward to, then, friends, you would not fear death but only embrace it, in all of its fulfilment.

Where thought is reality, imagine the thought of the things you wanted to do but for some reason could not do, but in the spirit world can now do.

On the earth plane, a lion would eat you, but in the world of spirit, a lion has no want for food. Result: you can cuddle it, without being its dinner.

I say again: imagine a world where the once impossible now becomes possible. Sounds good? Then let these words take away any fear of death, and rejoice in the new world and the new life to come.

Religion has drummed into us God's punishment. We have been taught to fear God, which in itself can be another reason to fear death.

But I say this: how can you fear such a beautiful god who loves all of his children equally?

In my mind, religion is man-made to put the fear of God into us if we go off the rails, for want of a better phrase.

Now, replace the word religion with the word spiritual, which is a beautiful relationship between us and our heavenly father who loves us all unconditionally, as we all should love one another.

We have been given free will; we will at times make mistakes, stray off the road sometimes, be lost and confused, etc., but trust me, God will never leave any of His children behind.

Now, when a child dies, our first thought is how can an all-loving god take our child from us? Well, first, let's go back to where I explained that death is not a punishment.

Most people for the majority of their lives think that they are only a physical being. Now, if you ask someone who has spiritual knowledge, they will put you right on this. We are spirit within a physical body, meaning a soul within.

And the soul has what you could call a "soul purpose".

And when the soul has achieved its purpose, it will leave the physical body, as the physical body is merely a vehicle from which the soul can express and fulfil its purpose.

So a soul or spirit, whatever way you wish to call it, may just want to know and experience what it is like just to be born into this world, i.e., incarnate. I like to call it just passing through, so it may return the same day back to the spirit world, meaning like a cot death, the spirit coming and returning.

To fully understand this is to understand reincarnation.

Some people have had a glimpse of the spirit world and know just what it is like to pass at the moment of death, by having what's called a near- death experience (NDE for short).

Those who have experienced this have reported that their fear of death has gone.

Many have said it has also changed their lives forever.

It is as if their view of life has opened up to a new level of understanding.

Many years ago, my brother John Alice suffered a heart attack, where for a short time he passed over because his heart had stopped beating. For a brief moment, he said he found himself floating above his physical body, watching the doctors trying to restart his heart. Then he found himself going through a long tunnel at a great speed, where he reported a bright beam of light, in which he saw and spoke to our grandmother, who said to him, 'Go back, John, as it is not time for you to pass over.' No sooner had she said those words than he found himself back inside his physical body, where the doctors were successful in restarting his heart.

And I would like to point out that up until then, my brother had no knowledge or belief in life after death. This changed his mind and he now has a belief in the spirit world and all its glory.

There are cases of near-death experiences where the person who had one was perhaps not a very nice person beforehand, selfish and unkind, and the result of having an NDE was becoming a better person, meaning being a more kind and thoughtful person, even taking on charity work.

Some say they have been given a second chance at life, and their friends and family find a change in them; where beforehand was one big negative challenge, now they are more positive in their outlook on life and have more drive.

Look at it from this point of view. You are standing on a beach, okay, pick up one grain of sand, then look around you and see how much sand is on that beach, and how many grains of sand it takes to make up that beach.

Now is it not the same with life itself? We only know just a small particle, for when we die, or pass, for want of a better word, our consciousness opens up to its full potential, seeing that the universe holds much more than our minds can even start to imagine.

Also, some who have had an NDE come back with messages in a bid to make a better world.

We can in my view really have heaven on earth. What I mean by that statement is, put an end to greed, power, violence, hate, etc., replacing these traits with kindness, compassion and tolerance, and learning the fine art of sharing.

God has provided every man, woman and child with enough food and shelter and fresh clean water ... enough for every living being on earth.

However, we have rich and poor, the haves and have-nots, it's only through man's greed that many suffer, but not only man. The animal kingdom has suffered the most, with man overpopulating and taking the land that once animals grazed on.

The oceans overfished and the pollution of man's waste; out of sight, out of mind. Only mankind himself can change this behaviour and lack of common sense.

As a medium, I feel it is very important for me to share a fact with you all: it is said by some religions that if you are gay or lesbian, etc., then you live in limbo, unable to enter the kingdom of heaven.

Also, it is said by some religions that if a person commits suicide, again, he will live in limbo, unable to enter the kingdom of heaven.

Well, newsflash, this is far from the truth. I have worked with the spirit world for many years, and I can say, hand on heart, I have brought through many spirits who have been gay or lesbian, and they are very much happy and alive in heaven.

As I too have brought through many spirits who have committed suicide. What must truly be understood here is that the world of spirit is love.

So why would an all-loving god punish someone for loving another? Whether it be a love between two men or two women, love is love; there is no judgement.

The same goes for someone taking their own life; ask a hundred mediums the same question and they will all tell you the same.

The doors to God's kingdom are open to all, through our lord Jesus Christ.

Even our beloved pets are there, will be there; only too happy to greet us on our return back home to the world of spirit.

I myself am looking forward to being greeted by my loved ones who have passed before me.

Try to understand that we are all spirit and always have been spirit and always will be spirit.

As well as near-death experiences, you also have what is an out-of- body experience (OBE for short). So what happens when you have an out-of-body experience?

We usually experience our conscious selves as located within our bodies, but when you have an out-of-body experience, it feels like your conscious self is separate and out of your physical body.

Out-of-body experiences are associated with a number of factors, including near-death experiences, sleep and medical conditions.

While different people have described out-of-body experiences in different ways, they generally report and agree that during an OBE, a person feels their consciousness is located outside of their physical body, or they experience a split self. While one part experiences a floating feeling of the world from that elevated perspective, a break in unity of the body, the self feels very real.

There are a number of circumstances and conditions that seem to make it more likely that people will have an OBE.

These can cause one of two kinds of OBE: spontaneous OBE or induced OBE.

Near-death experiences often happen if someone's heart stops for a time and their spirit leaves their body, but if they get their heart started in time, then the spirit will quickly return.

Your spirit can also leave your body and return while you are sleeping. Remember: the spirit is connected to your physical body by a thin silver cord.

Also, with certain medical conditions, such as poor mental health or brain injury, you can also have induced out-of-body experiences, which I will talk about in due course, called astral projection.

This also applies to drugs with hallucinogenic properties, such as ketamine, marijuana, heroin and LSD, and people under anaesthetic.

Astral projection is not something new; people from all over the world have reported doing it, and with their much lighter and more capable astral bodies, they are able to do mind-blowing things, including travelling to celestial planes of existence and interacting with a vast array of higher beings.

Remember: the real you is an immortal soul that has lived many different lifetimes on many different planes of existence; the real you lives on long after your current physical form expires. Learning astral projection puts the fear of death in a rear-view mirror.

Having an out-of-body experience is said to be life-changing. Astral projection allows you to have an out-of-body experience at will. Understanding that your consciousness exists forever really puts things into perspective.

This is just one lifetime of many, no need to be living in fear. Life dramas and personal conflicts naturally fall away; we are spiritual beings having a human experience. Knowing the truth helps us to appreciate our current life on a whole new level.

Essential to astral projection is learning to become more in tune with your mind and body, naturally developing a certain kind of skill and mastery in this way.

Awakening your mega-powerful subconscious and unconscious mind unlocks a wide variety of benefits, such as creativity, intuition and problem-solving.

(But, please, do not try to astral travel without proper training.)

Chapter Eleven

There is still more we can learn

God has given us

God has given us eyes to see.
To see the beauty in the world we live in.
The eyes to see the beauty in another.

God has given us a mouth to speak kind words, when someone needs them most, words of kindness and hope, words which guide and encourage someone to be the best version of themself.

God has given us shoulders to carry our heavy load, shoulders for someone to lean on and cry upon.

God has given us hands, to lift someone when they fall, hands to work and feed our families, hands to heal the sick, hands to touch people's hearts.

God has given us legs and feet, to walk that extra mile, and to run to the aid of another.

God has given us a heart, to show love and give love, and to understand love, to feel and express our feelings, hopes and desires.

God has given us a mind, a mind to choose and decide, to think and to understand, a mind to know right from wrong, to show compassion and empathy, a mind to show forgiveness and to reflect, to show gratitude in all the wonderful things we have in our lives.

Praise the lord for the body we have and the life he has given us all.

Praise the lord for the good times but most of all the bad times, as this is where we find strength, knowledge and spiritual understanding, for in darkness the light will shine the brightest.

Everything is temporary

Every moment, every situation and every belonging is temporary.

For yesterday will become today, then will become tomorrow in a moment of time.

When something serves us no more purpose, it simply ceases to be our life.

The best way I can explain this statement is by explaining how I look at possessions in my life.

Well, I look at it this way: I simply don't possess anything in my life. I'm just a caretaker of what you may call possessions; I don't own them, I just take care of them until they serve me no more purpose.

Our friends and families are only in our lives until they pass to the spirit world.

But saying that could be contradictory as they live on in our hearts and minds, and we will also see them again when we ourselves enter the world of spirit.

This also applies to the wonderful relationship I share with my beautiful fiancée, Michelle. We are in each other's lives not because we have to be but because we want to be in each other's lives.

We don't own or possess each other; we did not buy one another from a supermarket shelf.

We are two parts of a whole, both because we have a deep love and affection for each other and a spiritual bond.

Some relationships are built on a physical love and affection for each other, but Michelle's and mine is based on both a physical and a spiritual level.

Michelle, like me, is far from materialistic. I remember saying to Michelle, 'You really need to start zipping your handbag up, before someone puts their hand in and steals your purse.'

Well, a few months on, someone did steal her purse, to which she said, 'It's okay, Michael. Perhaps they needed the money more than me.'

And that is a true fact; sometimes, others' needs are greater than our own, resulting in the fact that if you lose something, it cannot effect you in any way, because you are only a caretaker looking after things until they serve no more purpose for you.

Do not be so quick to judge

The best way I can explain this is to use a scenario.

Okay, what I want you to do is imagine I take a group of, let's say, twenty people to an art gallery to look at a painting.

We all look at the painting from the same angle, resulting in only five percent liking the painting.

Now, this time, we all look at the same painting from all different angles, resulting in all twenty of us liking the painting, by simply looking from a different approach.

Now, let's see what happens when we apply this to our everyday lives.

Looking at people and things with an expanded open mind, looking at both sides of the coin, instead of just one side, perhaps we will not be so judgemental.

Self-reflection

Taking time to look back over my life, were the decisions I made in my life the right ones? If not, what should the decisions have been? Would they have made me a better man?

I remember watching the film *The Shawshank Redemption*, when Red, played by Morgan Freeman, is in front of the parole board and is asked, 'Have you changed and are you safe enough to be released back into society?'

And his reply was, 'Well, let me tell you this, Sonny, if I could go back in time, I would grab that young man I once was and shake him,' meaning don't go down that road.

Well, in one sense, I would do the same with the man I was all those years ago, but also I'm aware that I had to be that man I once was.

Okay, let me explain why I say this. Well, simply, I had to be that person, as much as I did not like him, for without being him, I could not have had all those experiences I went through, to help and guide and educate people not to go down the same avenues I once walked, and to share the spiritual knowledge I have gained, to guide them back onto the right road, without judgement.

Remember: spiritual growth and understanding are open and there for everyone.

But also be mindful that we all progress at different speeds, and we must all open our awareness and consciousness up to a higher level.

How I deal with situations in my life now is that I look at them from a spiritual perspective. How will my words and actions effect another in a positive way rather than a negative way? I try to put myself in their shoes.

One thing I'm a true believer of is karma; what goes around comes around. I should know this as karma has come back many times to bite me on my backside.

And also I'm a hugging person. My dad in the spirit world was not, and when he came through one time, he said he regretted not being able to show affection.

Change comes from within

High up in the Himalayan Mountains lives a spiritual guru. The only people he saw were tourists, and he would watch them eating their pizzas.

One day, the guru thought to himself, *I think I must try a pizza*. So, the next day, he came down from the mountain and walked into a pizza parlour and said to the cashier, 'How much is one of your pizzas?'

The cashier said, 'Ten dollars, sir.' With that, the guru gave the cashier a twenty-dollar bill.

When the pizza was cooked, the cashier gave the guru the pizza then walked off. 'Excuse me,' he said to the cashier, 'I gave you a twenty-dollar bill, and the pizza was ten dollars, so you owe me ten dollars' change.'

With that, the cashier said, 'Surely, sir, with you being a guru, you would understand that change comes from within.'

How poverty taught me to be humble

When I was around three years old, my mother, Kathleen, divorced my biological father, John, after ten years of marriage, leaving my mother to be a single parent, relying on state handout payments.

My father would not pay my mother maintenance towards the upbringing of my brother and me, which meant times were tough financially.

When the rent man called, I remember we all had to hide behind the settee without a sound, because he would try and look through the windows and the letterbox.

Our mother would often forsake a meal just to feed my brother and me. As for gas and electric, we had a meter, which took shillings in old money. We would often put our coats on our beds just to keep us warm.

We did not even have carpets around the house; we had old 1960s lino, which I can tell you was very cold under our feet in the wintertime.

One day, my brother John decided we should both go out and do some begging to help our mother, to put food on the table and shillings in the meter.

First, I must tell you that Gravesend is just across the London/Kent border, so our accent is the same as the London cockney accent. So here you have two young boys, wearing poor clothing, with cockney accents. We were like something out of *Oliver Twist*.

We would say in our cockney accents, 'Hey, mister, got any spare change, please, sir?'

Well, to our delight and astonishment, that day we made seventeen old pennies, which we put in an old Matchbox cars box and joyfully handed to our mother. Okay, so we got a good telling-off for begging, but at the same time our mother knew our good intentions came from two kind little hearts.

Now in Gravesend we have a very large Indian community. It has the nickname of Little India, mainly down to Idi Amin throwing the Asian community out of Uganda, and the poverty in India itself in places like Calcutta.

Now, every one of those seventeen old pennies was given to us by the Indian community; not one penny was given from our own white community.

And I will explain why: when you have experienced poverty first-hand, then you understand the feeling and worry it holds, and you never forget it, and you become more humble.

As time passed, my mother got remarried, to a certain William Russell, who became our stepfather and who owned his own house, left to him by his late mother, the house I will come back to after telling you all what happened a few years ago, which will tie together all that I'm saying.

Okay, a few years ago, when my granddaughter Jasmine Dermeechi was around nine years old, I asked her to do a few little jobs for me around my home. In return, I gave her a few pounds.

After she finished, we drove into town, where I knew there would be a homeless man sitting.

I said to Jasmine, 'See that homeless man sat there, he might not have a hot meal inside of him tonight, or even a bed to sleep in.' I said, 'How lucky we both are to have a nice hot meal and bed to sleep in tonight.

'So, Jasmine, you have a choice. You can buy some sweets with the money you have earned, or you can give it to the homeless man, to also help him to eat tonight. Remember, I'm not going to judge you either way as this is your choice and your choice alone.'

With that, she went over to the homeless man and said, 'Take this money to help you eat tonight.'

And the homeless man said, 'God bless you, girl.'

I then turned to Jasmine and said, 'How did that feel?'

With tears in her eyes, she said, 'Thank you, Grandad, that felt good,' and she still remembers that to this day.

Now, back to my mother and stepfather's house. Well, when my mother and Bill passed, the house was sold, and my brother and sister and I all got around £50,000 each.

After giving my offspring a share, I gave the rest to many charities.

So those few years of poverty as a young child helped me in my latter years, and I thank God for the experience of being poor as it taught me the value of what I have in life, and not what I don't have.

It also taught me about hard work. At the tender age of thirteen, I had a paper round, helped out on the milk float and worked down the local market. I even bought a pair of school shoes, costing £4.20, by doing penny for the guy.

Another thing I would like to say, and point out, is that when the kind Indian community gave me and my brother those seventeen old pennies, it was a time of racial unrest in the town. It was the days of National Front marches and parading through the town centre. They were persecuted for just trying to better their lives and live in a safer place.

Remember, this was only twenty years after partition between India and Pakistan, yet they gave their pennies to two poor young white boys, and I can say here and now that they gave from their hearts.

So may God's blessings be upon them and their families.

Here is another example of how hard work pays off in the end.

When my sons were young, they wanted a tent, which was twenty pounds to buy. In truth, I could have bought the tent outright.

However, I thought to myself, *hello, a lesson on the value of money could be taught here.*

'Okay,' I said, 'you can have a tent but you will be buying it, but I will also help you to do so.'

Now, at that time in the 1990s, the scrap value of aluminium was high, so for an aluminium Coke can, you could make one penny; so, in theory, we would need a lot of aluminium cans.

So, over a short space of time, my sons and I collected as many cans as we could find, then I took them to work and put them through the crusher (not the children by the way, it was the cans ... laugh).

Before long, we had enough in weight to take to the scrap yard, twenty pounds was paid out, and they bought their tent with the money they had earned.

So, two things happened: my sons got to know the way hard work pays off in the end, and we had a cleaner town in doing so.

And both sons own their own houses.

How I look today

Me doing Sunday Service

Me at the age when I went begging with my brother John to help our mother

The power of our thoughts

We should all be mindful of just how powerful our thoughts can be, for our thoughts can be the making of our happiness or our unhappiness, depending on whether they are positive or negative.

Our thoughts of today become our reality of our tomorrow.

As a medium, I have sceptics say to me that when we die there is nothing, just darkness. Well, I say this, be careful, because your thoughts will become your reality. If, like me, your thoughts on life after death are that you go to a better place, full of beauty, full of love, a place of compassion, a place where there is no judgement, bitterness or hatred, only love, then good news, this will become your reality.

Have you ever noticed that the things we do in life just seem to repeat themselves, over and over again, and we find we make the same old mistakes? The only way to change this pattern is to just simply change our thoughts.

I have known people to date or even marry the wrong kind of person, time after time, attracting the same sort of person with the same characteristics as the last person they were with.

There is one thing I think we would all agree on; it is that at some stage of our lives, we have all said the words *I'm in two minds to do it this way or that way.*

Well, I will tell you how I look at the mind.

I split my mind into two halves, never forgetting that two halves equal a whole. Okay, half of my mind is the physical mind; the other half is my spiritual mind. Now, sometimes, what we think is good for the physical is indeed harmful and non-productive for the soul, meaning the spiritual mind.

As an example, someone has upset you, and your thoughts have been given a choice as to how to deal with the situation, in a rational and positive way, or a spiteful, revengeful, negative way. I'm sure you will agree that the positive way would be the one your soul would better benefit from, regarding your spiritual growth.

Your inner thoughts control your gut feeling, your intuition. A thought pops into your mind; is this man or woman the right one for me? But something inside you is unsure. That is a warning signal from your intuition, telling you all is not well. Some will listen to their inner thoughts, and some will ignore them.

And there are times when we have to use our intuition to work out if our thoughts are true or not, as sometimes what we believe to be true is found to be the opposite.

I will endeavour to explain what I mean by this dilemma, which can leave you confused but relieved at the same time. For this, I will make up a scenario.

You have a thought come into your mind, that your wife or husband has been cheating on you.

Okay, over the course of a month, he or she has been going out a couple of times a week. You try texting and phoning them, but their phone just goes straight to voicemail, and all of this is out of character, so a negative way of thinking takes over.

But the truth is that your wedding anniversary is coming up and your partner cannot dance to save their life, so for a wonderful surprise, they have been taking dancing lessons, because they have arranged a romantic weekend away for you both, let's say to Blackpool, to sweep you off your feet on the dance floor.

I sent out a thought to God, saying, *I wish to write a book, to share my spiritual knowledge and to take away the fear of dying.* I said, *please inspire and guide me in your great wisdom.*

That is true and honest, even if it means that I bow my head in shame for the man I was before the awakening of my soul.

Now remember at the beginning of the book, I wrote I was once a very selfish and controlling man, a master of reverse psychology, manipulating someone's thoughts.

I thank God I'm not that man anymore, but I'm also thankful that I was that man. Let me explain why I say this. To have knowledge and understanding, first, you must live through the experience, from both sides of the spectrum.

Now remember how I have said that what comes around goes around, meaning the very same happened to me. I allowed someone to control me, my thoughts, my feelings, who I could speak to and what I could or could not do, and looking back, I'm so grateful to them for doing so. I feel no bitterness towards them, only heartfelt appreciation.

I was conducting a night of clairvoyance in which I said to a lady in the audience, 'I have your mother in spirit with me, and she's telling me you are letting your partner treat you like a doormat. He is dictating and controlling every aspect of your life, from the clothes you wear to the people you can and cannot speak to.' I said, 'Can you take what I'm saying?'

With a red face, she said, 'Yes, I can, thank you.'

Now here is where spiritual knowledge and experience come into play, as little did I know her partner was sat beside her.

After the meeting, I spoke to them both, more so the chap. I said, 'My friend, I'm not here to judge you, only to tell you that I was once like you, treating partners in the same way you are treating your good lady, and one day, just like me, you will look back and understand that it is not the way a lady, or even a man, should be treated.'

So I said, 'You have a choice. Carry on treating your wife the way you are, and take the risk of losing her, or treat her as your equal, letting her be herself, and growing together as one.

'Remembering the lady you fell in love with, why would you want to change her if you truly loved everything about her in the beginning?'

So can you see that by being that selfish, controlling, horrid person I was has helped many couples in their relationships years later? This is why I thank God so much for all the wonderful life experiences I have the good fortune to have had, and trust me, I'm still learning today.

One lesson I have learnt is from my beautiful fiancée, Michelle. Going back to the start of our relationship, Michelle pointed out to me, might I say in a loving way, 'Michael,' she said, 'I've noticed you say the word I a lot. May I ask how many people there are in this relationship?'

My reply was, 'Two, my love, why do you ask?'

'Well,' she replied, 'if there are two people in this relationship, why do you always say the word I? Should it not be the word we, meaning two of us, like, *shall we get a takeaway tonight for dinner?*'

Well, Michelle opened my eyes to something I was unaware of. When I thought about this, my first thought was how must this have made her feel? My darling Michelle must have felt excluded from the very relationship she was in.

Well, I can say that nowadays I use the word we, and our relationship has grown from strength to strength, so the right thoughts can improve and enrich our lives.

Spiritual thoughts far outweigh materialistic thoughts. Why do I say this? Well, if I went back thirty years and I was walking down the road and there was a fifty-pound note on the floor, I would have picked it up and straight away, without any thought for the owner, I would have put it in my back pocket. Now the spiritual person I am today would think of the owner and hand it in at the police station.

Okay, so a thought comes into your mind. What happens next is that your thinking mechanism kicks in: how do I react to this thought? Well, first, decide whether it is a positive or negative thought. I would like to say sometimes it would be mindful to keep some thoughts to oneself.

I will explain why I say this. Well, as I've said sometimes, a thought can result in negative thinking, in a way of thinking that something is true, but, however, it is wrong. As a result, we deal with it in a negative and self-destructive way.

I will give you an example. A few people got a thought in their mind, which got them thinking, and they put their thoughts on Facebook. What they thought was fact was far away from the truth. What can I say; the damage was done. It destroyed me and also the trust I have in people, resulting in me having anxiety and panic attacks, so now I have mental health issues.

The sad thing is that it has affected so many wonderful people, because I used social media to send out healing and spiritual advice to anyone who needed it.

So the best advice I can give anyone is, think before you act on a thought. Is it a positive or a negative one?

Sometimes, our minds become clogged up with thoughts and this would be a good time for you to meditate, to give your overworked mind a good rest.

While we are on the subject of the power of our thoughts, a thought just entered my mind that I wish to share with you all, a very funny and uplifting one, when a wonderful spirit left me lost for words in a positive way.

I was conducting an evening of clairvoyants at my local spiritualist church. I must point out it was on a Sunday, which is a divine service, which meant I was more conservative in the way I was working.

I said to a lady in the congregation, 'My darling I have your friend with me in the spirit world. May I work with you, please?'

'Yes, that will be fine,' she said. Now, I was aware the spirit was standing to the left of me, so I turned around to her, to talk telepathically, where she transmits her thoughts into my mind.

To my shock and surprise, she lifted up her top, exposing her breasts to me, and she burst out laughing. Saying to myself, *how am I going to put this across in a Sunday service?* I just stood there for a moment. How could I say to the lady in the congregation that her friend had just shown me her breasts, and the spirit laughed, saying, *get out of this one, Michael.*

Well, I turned to the lady and could not talk for a moment, but the lady could see by my red face what her friend in spirit had done. She burst out laughing, saying, 'I bet my friend has just flashed her breasts at you. Don't worry,' she said, 'she was forever getting them out when she was on the earth plane. Well done,' she said, 'good evidence.'

You see, when we return to the world of spirit, we take with us our personality, our essence, our characteristics, meaning who we were as a person. So when we pass (like the spirit who flashed me), we certainly hold on to our sense of humour, as spirits will use any method possible to prove it really is them and that life truly is eternal to every human being.

One positive thing we can take from our thoughts is that they can evoke memories of our lives, happy times in our lives, funny times we have had, which can turn a sad moment into a happy one.

Like I say to everyone who is going through a hard time in their life, think of the worst thing they have had to deal with, such as the loss of a loved one. Somehow, they got through it. Life is like a fairground roller coaster; there will be ups and downs in our lives, and we can and will overcome them.

When we take a train journey, the train enters many tunnels on its way to its destination, some short and some long tunnels, but as we all know, there is always light at the end of the tunnel, so have faith that you will overcome any situation as everything is only temporary.

For you may not understand at the time, but God will not give us anything we cannot handle and overcome. Sometimes, it's only our thoughts leading us to think we cannot.

Never in a million years would I have thought all those years ago that one day I would become a medium, and never would I have thought I'd write a book on my spiritual knowledge. I have learnt to help others.

But it just goes to show that anyone can turn their life around for the better. As I've said, progression is open to every human being.

It has taken some time to write this book. I would write for a while and then I would do other things in my life, so in the end I had to apply some discipline and lock myself away from the outside world for a while.

Never in a million years would I have believed the world-famous medium and spiritual teacher and author of so many spiritual books would come through me, using me as an instrument, meaning medium, to give my Michelle a message, not just once but a few times now. How lucky and blessed I feel at this stage of my life.

Now I know when this book is published, it is going to do well.

Why do I say this? Well, because my intentions are honourable, meaning I'm not writing it for material gain.

As my reward is the love of God and doing God's work, remember what Jesus said: you worship God or money as you cannot worship both.

If your thoughts are with the intention of helping others, God will guide you along that path. I will give you all an example of how this works.

Both Michelle and I like to go down to the coast. I love to go on the machines where I can win keyrings for the family and I seem to do well.

Now, Michelle plays on the slot machines and wins every time she plays them. Now, Michelle can walk away with over a hundred pounds or more at a time.

Now I will give you the reason why she wins so much. It's because her first thought is what she's going to do with the winnings. Well, her intentions are honourable, as she gives every pound of what she wins to charity.

I remember, as a child, my mother saying to me, 'Michael, always respect your elders.'

Now I'm an elder, I have a greater understanding of what she meant by the statement, for with age comes wisdom, because as I've said many times, to have knowledge and understanding, first there must be experience.

Along the road my children and grandchildren are walking, the mistakes, situations and challenges they are facing are the ones I myself had to work out and overcome.

That is why we have the saying *mother knows best*; good advice to a daughter who is having a baby. Ask your mother, turn to your mother, as she has knowledge of the experience.

The elders' spiritual leaders of the indigenous people, and elders of the gypsy community, pass their wisdom down to the next generation, having gained their wisdom through their experiences.

Now, we have all heard the biblical saying *we reap what we sow*.

So elders plant a seed in the minds of the next generation, to spread their wisdom and guidance of what they learnt from their own experiences, for when you plant a seed, in time it will germinate and grow, and over time, it will bear fruit.

And in time the young themselves will become elders, giving their knowledge and wisdom, so always be mindful and respect your elders.

Reincarnation

Reincarnation is the religious or philosophical belief that the soul or spirit, after biological death, begins a new life in a new body that may be human, animal or spiritual, depending on the moral quality of the previous life's actions.

Here are just a few stories of cases where people have been reincarnated.

'When I was your age, I changed your diaper,' said the young boy to his father. Ron looked down on his smiling son, who had not yet turned two.

He thought it was a strange thing to say, but he figured he had misheard him.

But, as a baby, Sam made similar remarks over the next few months. Ron and his wife, Cathy, gradually pieced together an old story. Sam believed that he was his deceased grandfather, Ron's late father, who had returned to his family. More intrigued than alarmed, Ron and Cathy asked Sam, 'How did you come back?'

'I just went whoosh and came out of the portal,' he responded.

Although Sam was a precocious child – he had been speaking in full sentences from the age of eighteen months – his parents were stunned to hear him use a word like portal, and they encouraged him to say more.

They asked Sam if he'd had any siblings, and he replied that he had a sister who turned into a fish.

'Who turned her into a fish?' asked his father.

'Some bad guys,' she said.

Eerily enough, Sam's grandfather had a sister who had been murdered sixty years earlier. Her body was found floating in San Francisco Bay.

Ron and Cathy then gently asked Sam, 'Do you know how you died?' Sam jerked back and slapped the top of his head as if in pain. One year before Sam was born, his grandfather died of a cerebral haemorrhage.

Vladimir Levinski, who was born David Secombe in England in 1930, had such an innate gift for playing the piano that he was able to teach himself to be a concert pianist. (When asked about lessons, he remarked, 'I have no time for them. I have a technique of my own.') So gifted was Levinski, and at such a young age, that he came to recognise himself as the reincarnation of Franz Liszt, the Hungarian composer and pianist.

By the age of twenty-one, he was performing for packed concert halls and known as the Paganini of the piano. Unfortunately, Levinski's interest in Liszt at times came to border on obsession, such as when he was playing a concert on 23rd January 1952, and stopped playing halfway through to talk about Liszt.

The audience were disappointed, but Levinski, for his part, felt the concert was a tremendous success, in part because he experienced it as only the reincarnation of the renowned composer and performer Liszt could.

Mommy, I'm so homesick

Among the UVA case studies is the story of an Oklahoma boy named Ryan.

A few years ago, the four-year-old woke up screaming at two in the morning. Over the preceding months, he'd been pleading with his bewildered mother, Cyndi, to take him to the house where he'd lived before.

In tears, he'd beg her to return him to his glittering life in Hollywood, complete with a big house, pool and fast cars. It was so fabulous that he once said, 'I can't live in these conditions. My last home was much better.'

When Cyndi went into her son's room that night, Ryan kept repeating the same words – 'Mommy, I'm homesick' – as she tried to comfort him and rock him to sleep.

'He was like a little old man who couldn't remember all the details of his life, he was so frustrated and sad,' Cyndi said.

The next morning, she went to the library, borrowed a pile of books about old Hollywood and brought them home. With Ryan on her lap, Cyndi went through the volumes, and she was hoping the pictures might soothe him.

Instead, he became more and more excited as they looked at one particular book. When they came to a still of a scene from a 1932 movie called *Night after Night,* he stopped her.

'Mama,' he shouted, pointing to one of the actors, who wasn't identified, 'that guy's me! The old me!'

'I was shocked,' Cyndi admitted. 'I never thought that we'd find the person he thought he was,' but she was equally relieved.

'Ryan had talked about his other life and been so unhappy, and now we had something to go on.'

Although neither Cyndi nor her husband believed in reincarnation, she went back to the library the next day and checked out a book about children possessing memories of their past lives.

This is a very interesting story of reincarnation. It occurred in 1957 in England.

It is the story of Joanna (aged eleven) and Jacqueline Pollock (aged six), sisters who suffered a car accident in which they were run over near the pavement and died.

Mrs Pollock became pregnant one year after the date of the accident and her husband told her he had a hunch that this birth would bring twin girls who were their daughters, the same who had died a year before.

The odd thing was that the gynaecologist who treated Mrs Pollock said he did not expect more than one baby, but Mrs Pollock finally had two girls; these were called Jennifer and Gillian.

The girl's father noticed that one of the babies had, above her right eyebrow, a scar identical to that of their daughter Jacqueline, who had fallen when she was three, and the other girl in turn had a mole the size of a thumb, in the same place as their second deceased daughter.

Four months later, the family moved to another village, but after two and a half years they went back to visit the same place where they was born, and their parents found that the two girls knew the place very well, even without seeing the school.

They could point a finger to where it was, and the same thing happened when they pointed to the place where the swing and slide were. When the girls went through their old house, they recognised every place immediately.

When the girls turned four, their father opened the box in which he kept their dead daughters' old toys. The strange thing for the parents was that each girl acknowledged which toy belonged to who, and even called the dolls by the names the deceased sisters had used, but also the girls showed a fear of passing cars and personally behaved in the same way as their dead daughters had previously.

Many years ago, I had a past life regression. For this to happen, I had to go into a deep meditative state, where I saw myself as a member of the opposite sex, a female in Victorian times, getting out of a horse-drawn carriage. I was dressed in a white silk evening dress. My husband was a doctor, similar in looks to Prince Michael of Kent, same white beard and dress code. We were spending the night at the opera, then I woke up.

Ask yourself these questions.

Do you have a fear of water? If so, did you drown in a past life?

Do you have a fear of flying? If so, did you die in a plane crash in a past life?

Do you have a fear of fire? If so, did you die in a fire in a past life?

Are you a man or a woman and you feel you are trapped in the wrong body? If so, were you a member of the opposite sex in a past life?

Do you have a fear of closed spaces? If so, did you die in a cave or down a coal mine?

Do you have a fear of open spaces? If so, did you die on a battlefield?

Have you met a person you have never met before, but you feel you have known them all your life? Could they have been a friend or a family member in a past life?

You know a foreign language, but you have never been taught it, or even been to the country, but somehow you find you can speak it. Did you live there in a past life?

It sure gets you thinking.

I will now talk a little bit about what's called the Akashic records.

Spiritual enlightenment and scientific theory clash in the realm of light that holds the answer to all things past, present and future.

This almost unobtainable book is filled with thoughts, emotions, motivations, actions and even prophecies.

Future life matters are not written in stone, so to speak; they are constantly changing based upon one's actions and reactions throughout their lifetime.

While different cultures and individuals call these records by various names, science may have uncovered a physical space in which they exist, or at the very least a place that provides us with a bridge or channel to their access.

It is ultimately through the Akashic records that only a select few have been able to experience such a supreme state of enlightenment and spiritual growth.

While not impossible, meditation can provide an avenue, but only to those most practised and open to cardinal experiences.

While visions of fancy for some, there is nothing wrong with literally reaching for the stars in practices of enlightenment and fulfilment.

It is the cosmic databank where the truth of all that ever was, is and will be stored.

It is basically all the things that ever happened to a person or to a soul. So whatever was part of your journey, whatever you've experienced, all your impressions, everything is stored there in that field of information.

When you access the Akashic records, you can either have just pure insight-read only, or you can use that information to transform your energy, and accordingly, there will be a change made in the Akashic records.

Let's say I find out that I have a really huge fear of drowning, because I've drowned multiple times in other lifetimes.

So if I then work on that, or I release the fear and panic and I do some transformation around that, then the Akashic records change accordingly.

*

As this book comes to a close, it just leaves me to say that I hope that it has opened your minds and hearts to the wonderful world of spirit.

And I hope it has given you insight and taken away any fear of when it is your turn to pass, and remember that when you picked up this book, it was not by chance; it was God's guidance, through which you were seeking answers and spiritual knowledge.

May God's love and blessing be with you all.

Michael Dermeechi

Milton Keynes UK
Ingram Content Group UK Ltd.
UKHW010643021023
429777UK00001B/10